A Fun Den

Written by Charlotte Raby
Illustrated by Noopur Thakur

Collins

bell

mud

• • •

bell

mud

a big log

red bugs

• • • • • • •

a big log

red bugs

a fun den

a big hug

a fun den

a big hug

/u/

/b/

Review: After reading

Use your assessment from hearing the children read to choose any GPCs and words that need additional practice.

Read 1: Decoding

- Turn to page 2 and ask the children to read the word **bell**. Check that they sound out the "ll" as /l/.
- Turn to page 7 and cover the "s" in the word **bugs**. Ask the children to read the word. Then uncover the "s" and ask the children to read the word again, ensuring they sound the "s" correctly as /z/.
- Turn to the "I spy sounds" pages (14–15) and take it in turns to point to an object, name it, and say whether the word has a /u/ or /b/ sound in it, or neither. Ask the children: Where is the umbrella? (*under the tree*). Point out the /u/ sound in the word under. Next ask: Which way up is the bat? (*upside down*). Again, point out the /u/ sound in the word upside. Can the children name the items that contain the /b/ or /u/ sound anywhere in the word? (*umbrella, bugs, butterflies, mushrooms; badger, bat, bike, bees, birds, branches*)

Read 2: Vocabulary

- Look back through the book and discuss the pictures. Encourage the children to talk about details that stand out for them. Use a dialogic talk model to expand on their ideas and recast them in full sentences as naturally as possible.
- Work together to expand vocabulary by naming objects in the pictures that children do not know.
- On pages 10 and 11, ask the children which word shows that they are having a good time with the den (***fun***) and which word shows that two people are being kind to each other (***hug***).

Read 3: Comprehension

- Turn to page 10 and look at the den being built. Ask what each family member is doing. Encourage the children to talk about their own experiences. Ask: Have you ever built a den? Where was it? Who did you build it with? What did you use?
- Using pages 14–15, invite the children to tell you about any items that appeared in the book.